WORKBOOK

FOR

The Body Keeps the Score

Brain, Mind, and Body in the Healing of Trauma

Exponential Growth

Copyright © 2022 by Exponential Growth
All rights reserved.

This workbook aims to provide accurate and trustworthy information on the subject and problem addressed. The sales pitch for a publication implies that the publisher is not necessary to provide appropriate accounting services that are authorized legal services. If professional or legal guidance is required, a skilled Person in the profession ought to be gotten from a recognized and endorsed Declaration of Principles by an American Bar Association Committee and a Committee of Associations and publishers.

It is not permitted to duplicate, copy, or transfer any portion of this either electronically or in paper form, this document. It is highly forbidden to record this publication, and the publisher must be contacted in writing before storing this material.

It is claimed that the information presented here is accurate and Consistent in that any responsibility, whether for negligence or another reason, by the use or exploitation of any rules, procedures, or instructions. The entire and exclusive responsibility of the author is included within.

All copyrights not owned by the publisher are owned by the respective authors. The material provided here is provided exclusively for informative reasons. The information is presented without a contract or any sort of warranty or promise.

Disclaimer and Use Policy

This publication may include product names, logos, brands, and other trademarks that are the property of its respective they are not associated with Knowledge Tree and are trademark owners. The Publisher and author disclaims any guarantees or claims with regard to the veracity and comprehensiveness of these materials and disclaims all guarantees, including those of fitness for a specific purpose. This manual is unapproved and unofficial. Not at all the original book's author, approved, licensed, or endorsed by any licensees or affiliates of the author or publisher.

TABLE OF CONTENT

HOW TO USE THIS WORKBOOK 5

INTRODUCTION 8

INJURY 10
    KEY LESSONS 12
    KEY IDEAS FROM THIS SECTION IN YOUR OWN WORDS 13
    SELF-REFLECTION QUESTIONS 13
    ACTION PLAN 15

FLASHBACKS 16
    KEY LESSONS 18
    KEY IDEAS FROM THIS SECTION IN YOUR OWN WORDS 19
    SELF-REFLECTION QUESTIONS 19
    ACTION PLAN 21

YOUTH INJURY 22
    KEY LESSONS 24
    KEY IDEAS FROM THIS SECTION IN YOUR OWN WORDS 25
    SELF-REFLECTION QUESTIONS 25
    ACTION PLAN 27

RECOLLECTING MEMORIES 28
    KEY LESSONS 31
    KEY IDEAS FROM THIS SECTION IN YOUR OWN WORDS 32
    SELF-REFLECTION QUESTIONS 32
    ACTION PLAN 34

EMDR 35
    KEY LESSONS 38
    KEY IDEAS FROM THIS SECTION IN YOUR OWN WORDS 39
    SELF-REFLECTION QUESTIONS 39
    ACTION PLAN 41

YOGA 42
    KEY LESSONS 44
    KEY IDEAS FROM THIS SECTION IN YOUR OWN WORDS 45

    Self-Reflection Questions 45
    Action Plan 47

TAKING CARE 48
    Key Lessons 50
    Key Ideas from this section in your own words 51
    Self-Reflection Questions 51
    Action Plan 53

NEUROFEEDBACK 54
    Key Lessons 56
    Key Ideas from this section in your own words 57
    Self-Reflection Questions 57
    Action Plan 59

CONCLUSION 60

FINAL SELF-EVALUATION QUESTIONS 61

HOW TO USE THIS WORKBOOK

Hey there!
It is wonderful to see that you are interested in this workbook. This book is possibly one of the greatest in terms of habit formation and self-improvement formation. Filled with practical ideas that are easy to implement tips for forming healthy habits and knocking out harmful ones to be such an easy task!
The purpose of this workbook is to strengthen and emphasize the concepts and notions presented, making it far simpler for you to take action and use the knowledge you have gained from the book for practical, everyday use.

Using this worksheet will make it much simpler for you to take the next step in improving and increasing your productivity. You'll receive step-by-step instructions to become comfortable with little things in life. To acquire the knowledge you must respond to all the questions in a thorough manner to have a lasting influence and genuinely respond to the inquiries in the workbook. You can only do this by asking probing questions and providing sincere responses. Shed light on your priorities and take advantage of the opportunity to make long-lasting improvements in your daily life.

Additionally, the workbook will have significant summaries which are essential to understanding how to respond to the included queries. Consequently, for those who are limited by time, you are not necessarily needed to read the main book first to respond to the inquiries in this workbook. All the key points have been distilled and focused on for your understanding. For those who have read the book already, the previously mentioned key points will work effectively as brief reminders.

Please take your time and carefully read the workbook before beginning any of the questions in it. This section is one where careful reading can take the place of hurried reading.

The workbook contains the following;
1. Summaries of key areas of the book.
2. Key Lessons from the book
3. Key ideas from each section in your own words
4. Self-reflection questions
5. Action plan

You can easily follow up from the generated ideas which help your creativity in catching up and providing relevant answers to the questions therein, hence, giving you exponential growth in different aspects of your life.

I hope you find this useful and satisfying.

INTRODUCTION

The Body Keeps the Score makes sense of what injury is and the way that it can transform us for the more awful. These flickers examine the far-reaching impacts experienced by damaged individuals yet in addition to everyone around them. In any case, while injury presents various difficulties, there are ways of mending it.

How do you think this might benefit you? Figure out what injury means for your body and psyche. We know about accounts of damaged war veterans who have encountered savagery and torment, who have killed others during battle, or who have seen the passing of an individual fighter. Frequently, damaged troopers can't track down their direction back into society. They battle with their recollections, foster overly sensitive responses, and become aliens to themselves and their friends and family.

What occurs in the body and psyche of individuals who have encountered injury? Also, for what reason is it so hard to track down alleviation from it?

In these flickers, you'll realize the reason why awful encounters torment us. You'll figure out how injury patients see their current circumstances. At long last, you'll realize the reason why there's potential for damaged individuals and how injury can be recuperated.

You'll likewise find out
• why war veterans just trust other conflict veterans;
• why a standard picture in a magazine can set off shocking considerations; and
• how yoga lets injury patients free from their aggravation.

INJURY

Injury is staggeringly normal in our general public.

Injury isn't simply something looked at by war veterans - it's more common in our general public than we understand. Injury can happen to anybody, and it's time we figured out what this truly implies.

Injuries resulting from an encounter of intense pressure or agony that leaves a singular inclination vulnerable, or excessively wrecked, to adapt to misfortune. Encounters including war normally bring about injuries, however, savage violations and mishaps cause them as well.

Assault and kid misuse are horrible occasions, and they are additionally sadly surprisingly normal. Reports uncover that 12 million ladies were casualties of assault in the United States in 2014 alone and that more than 50% of those ladies were younger than 15 at the hour of the attack. Consistently in the United States, there are 3 million instances of youngster misuse.

These horrendous encounters can change the existences of those impacted, as well as the existences of their loved ones. Damaged individuals frequently experience the ill effects of post-horrible pressure issues (PTSD), which can prompt wretchedness and substance misuse.

Also, damaged individuals will quite often doubt anybody who hasn't encountered similar enduring they have and expect that no one can grasp them. This was shown in one of the treatment bunches the creator set up for Vietnam veterans.

While the gathering assisted the veterans with finding companions and offering their encounters, the individuals who weren't damaged by the conflict were viewed as pariahs by the gathering - including the creator. It required a long time of tuning in, relating to building entrust with the veterans for them to acknowledge him.

Laying out compatibility with somebody experiencing PTSD is a test all alone, so envision attempting to keep a marriage, a dear companionship, or a steady parent-kid relationship. Damaged individuals find it hard to trust even the people who love them most, including accomplices and children. This can be extremely hard on loved ones, frequently prompting alienation or separation.

Key Lessons

- Injury isn't simply something looked at by war veterans - it's more common in our general public than we understand.
- Damaged individuals frequently experience the ill effects of post-horrible pressure issues (PTSD), which can prompt wretchedness and substance misuse.
- Damaged individuals find it hard to trust even the people who love them most, including accomplices and children.
- Envision attempting to keep a marriage, a dear companionship, or a steady parent-kid relationship.

Key Ideas from this section in your own words

_____
_____
_____
_____
_____

Self-Reflection Questions

Draw out two questions from this section of the book and provide answers to the questions based on your study.

Question 1:
....
....

Answer_____
_____
_____
_____
_____

Question 2:
....
....

Answer_____

Action Plan

How do you intend to put the lessons from this section of the book into practice to improve your life?

_____
_____
_____
_____
_____
_____
_____
_____
_____
_____

FLASHBACKS

Flashbacks make individuals remember the psychological and actual experience of injury when they're helped to remember it.

At any point do you remember something humiliating you did and feel yourself wriggle or blush? Then, at that point, you have a small understanding of what recollections of injury can mean for the body.

At the point when a PTSD victim is helped to remember their injury, their body and cerebrum enter a high-stress mode, since they experience the memory as though it were genuine. This is known as a flashback, an effect of injury that the creator concentrated on in an examination he did with his patients.

Every patient consented to pay attention to a recording of content that reproduced their horrible experience. As the content played, members breathed in the air with a small convergence of radioactive particles. This air would be noticeable in a cerebrum filter, permitting the creator to see which regions of the mind were dynamic when patients recollected their injuries.

Marsha, a 40-year-old instructor, was first up for the investigation. Her content returned her to the shocking mishap that made her lose both her five-year-old little girl and the unborn youngster she was pregnant with at that point.

As Marsha stood by listening to the content, her circulatory strain and pulse rose strongly. Action in the left 50% of her cerebrum, the side answerable for levelheaded reasoning, dialed back and successfully "deactivated." A deactivation like this makes it challenging for PTSD victims to understand that the things they hear, see, and feel during a flashback aren't genuine.

In Marsha's cerebrum, Broca's region, the region liable for talking, showed a critical decline in action, leaving her unfit to talk. Her pressure

chemical levels shot up and remained high. For the intellectually sound, stress chemicals will spike and afterward decline when the danger has passed. Yet, for those with injury from quite a while ago, these chemicals take significantly longer to get back to typical levels.

This demonstrates that being helped to remember injury can be nearly essentially as sickening as encountering what is going on itself.

Key Lessons

- Flashbacks make individuals remember the psychological and actual experience of injury when they're helped to remember it.
- At the point when a PTSD victim is helped to remember their injury, their body and cerebrum enter a high-stress mode, since they experience the memory as though it were genuine.
- For the intellectually sound, stress chemicals will spike and afterward decline when the danger has passed.
- Being helped to remember injury can be nearly essentially as sickening as encountering what is going on itself.

Key Ideas from this section in your own words

_____
_____
_____
_____
_____

Self-Reflection Questions

Draw out two questions from this section of the book and provide answers to the questions based on your study.

Question 1:
....
....

Answer_____
_____
_____
_____
_____

Question 2:
....
....

Answer_____

Action Plan

How do you intend to put the lessons from this section of the book into practice to improve your life?

_____
_____
_____
_____
_____
_____
_____
_____
_____
_____

YOUTH INJURY

Youth injury has pessimistic effects, on an individual's childhood as well into adulthood, as well.

Horrible encounters are sufficiently hard to manage as a grown-up, however, there isn't anything more troublesome than confronting injury as a small kid. With minds that aren't even completely evolved, youngsters who go through an injury are at a more serious gamble to encounter a large number of unfortunate results. These outcomes surface in the years quickly following their encounters and later in adulthood.

Damaged youngsters frequently anticipate that awful things should occur. The creator exhibited this in an examination in which cards with pictures from magazines were displayed to youngsters who had encountered injury, and to the people who hadn't.

One of the cards showed two kids watching their dad fix a vehicle as he lay under it. While youngsters without injury envisioned a story in light of the picture where the dad effectively fixed the vehicle and took his children to Mcdonald's, the damaged kids envisioned a lot hazier situations.

One young lady said that one of the kids in the pictures would crush the dad's head with the sled he was holding. Another youngster said the vehicle would fall, squashing the dad's body. For these youngsters, the photos contained various triggers that drove them to envision the scene finishing viciously.

These reasoning examples frequently continue into adulthood.

Take Marilyn, one of the creator's patients and a previous medical caretaker. She told the creator she had a cheerful youth, yet this wasn't correct. Marilyn was physically mishandled as a kid, a horrendous encounter that molded her life as a grown-up.

She was inclined to suddenly erupt when men contacted her, even in her rest. She likewise fostered an immune system sickness that harmed her vision, which probably arose because of the pressure her injury caused on her body.

Marilyn's case might sound limited, yet she isn't the only one. Numerous other people who were damaged as youngsters keep on experiencing this in their grown-up lives.

Key Lessons

- Youth injury has pessimistic effects, on an individual's childhood as well into adulthood
- Horrible encounters are sufficiently hard to manage as a grown-up, however, there isn't anything more troublesome than confronting injury as a small kid.
- Youngsters who go through an injury are at a more serious gamble to encounter a large number of unfortunate results.
- If you can avoid injury, do all you have to in order to avoid it.

Key Ideas from this section in your own words

_____
_____
_____
_____
_____
_____

Self-Reflection Questions

Draw out two questions from this section of the book and provide answers to the questions based on your study.

Question 1:
....
....

Answer_____
_____
_____
_____
_____
_____

Question 2:
....
....

Answer_____

Action Plan

How do you intend to put the lessons from this section of the book into practice to improve your life?

_____
_____
_____
_____
_____
_____
_____
_____
_____
_____

RECOLLECTING MEMORIES

While ordinary recollections blur and change, horrible recollections are striking, perpetual, and effortlessly set off.

At the point when we recount stories, we will generally decorate, overstate or discard portions of our encounters. By the fifth time you've recounted a story, odds are good that it'll be very not quite the same as the principal variant. We even recall things distinctively over the long haul. Why would that be?

As a general rule, we won't quite often remember the tangible subtleties of occasions. The vast majority of us recollect what we did or how we felt by and large, yet don't store striking recollections about the smell of the room we were in or the specific subtleties of somebody's face. In any case, it's an alternate story with regards to horrible recollections - we recall these circumstances strikingly, and the recollections don't change over the long haul.

The creator exhibited the contrast between these two different ways of recollecting by requesting that members review significant yet nontraumatic occasions in their lives, similar to the introduction of their kid or their big day. In these cases, members could review their overall sentiments, similar to joy or apprehension, yet they didn't have an itemized picture of how their accomplice's hair took a gander at their marriage, for example.

Notwithstanding, when members were approached to review horrible recollections, smell, taste, contact, and hearing assumed an undeniably more significant part. One member who was assaulted said that a particular smell of liquor helped her in a split second to remember her injury, to such an extent that she was unable to hit up parties any longer.

We additionally review horrendous recollections reliably, without changes or corrections. In a review led at Harvard Medical School, 200 men were tried

consistently from their most memorable joining the examination, which they did somewhere in the range of 1939 and 1945, up until the current day. The subject of these tests was their recollections, and how injury, or scarcity in that department, formed them.

Numerous members were World War II veterans and resulting PTSD victims. While the recollections of members who weren't damaged by the conflict changed after some time, the veterans' recollections didn't change by any stretch of the imagination. They stayed reliable for well north of 45 years after the conflict finished.

Injury stays with you, both in your body and your cerebrum. So how do individuals figure out how to live with it?

Key Lessons

- At the point when we recount stories, we will generally decorate, overstate or discard portions of our encounters.
- As you recount a story probably for the fifth time, odds are that it'll not be quite the same as the principal variant.
- We additionally review horrendous recollections reliably, without changes or corrections.
- Injury stays with you, both in your body and your cerebrum.
- While ordinary recollections blur and change, horrible recollections are striking, perpetual, and effortlessly set off.

Key Ideas from this section in your own words

_____
_____
_____
_____
_____
_____

Self-Reflection Questions

Draw out two questions from this section of the book and provide answers to the questions based on your study.

Question 1:
....
....

Answer_____
_____
_____
_____
_____
_____

Question 2:
....
....

Answer

Action Plan

How do you intend to put the lessons from this section of the book into practice to improve your life?

_____
_____
_____
_____
_____
_____
_____
_____
_____
_____
_____

EMDR

EMDR permits patients to coordinate their recollections and reestablishes a feeling of organization over their psyche and body.

It might sound basic, yet quite possibly the best strategy the creator utilizes includes just a finger getting to and fro across a patient's field of vision. While the patient follows the finger with their eyes, they're directed through a horrendous memory and urged to make a new relationship en route.

This procedure is known as EMDR, or eye development desensitization and going back over.
While EMDR might sound adequately straightforward, there is some secret encompassing it, since little is had some significant awareness of how or why it's so successful. What is clear, in any case, is that it helps patients by coordinating horrendous recollections.

This is significant, since, supposing that recollections aren't coordinated, they can in any case work out before the eyes of a PTSD patient as though it's occurring progressively. When memory is coordinated, it can at last turn into one more previous occasion in the existence of a patient and stop having an upsetting unique kind of energy.

EMDR, similarly to different methods portrayed in these flickers, help a patient control their relationship to horrible mishaps by permitting them to coordinate it into their recollections. In doing as such, the patient can foster a new and better relationship with a horrendous memory, alongside a feeling of command over their brain, body, and life.

Shocking outcomes have been accomplished through EMDR.

Quite a while back, Kathy moved toward the creator at 21 years old, after having recently endeavored self-destruction for the third time. Kathy had been constrained into prostitution by her dad, during which time she'd been assaulted by her dad and his companions and physically attacked with brew bottles.

With the assistance of EMDR, Kathy had the option to notice her horrendous recollections and repackage them in a manner that gave her organization over them. The way into this cycle was that the meetings permitted her to bring a new, creative relationship to the surface.

For instance, during one meeting she envisioned a tractor pounding her life as a youngster home, obliterating the location of such countless horrendous recollections. In another, she envisioned keeping her dad out of a bistro, causing him to feel powerless and watching everybody around him giggle.

After eight meetings of headway like this, Kathy made a momentous recuperation. Furthermore, after 15 years, when the creator reconnected with Kathy, he was glad to see a solid and blissful lady who was thinking about embracing a third youngster.

Key Lessons

- When memory is coordinated, it can at last turn into one more previous occasion in the existence of a patient and stop having an upsetting unique kind of energy.
- EMDR helps a patient control their relationship to horrible mishaps by permitting them to coordinate it into their recollections.
- **EMDR** helps patients by coordinating horrendous recollections.

Key Ideas from this section in your own words

_____
_____
_____
_____
_____

Self-Reflection Questions

Draw out two questions from this section of the book and provide answers to the questions based on your study.

Question 1:
....
....

Answer_____
_____
_____
_____
_____

Question 2:
....
....

Answer_____

Action Plan

How do you intend to put the lessons from this section of the book into practice to improve your life?

_____
_____
_____
_____
_____
_____
_____
_____
_____
_____

YOGA

Yoga offers injury victims a protected method for investigating the connection between their body and brain.

Our body and psyche share a cozy relationship. To carry on with a fair, stable life, we want to comprehend how our feelings work, and what they mean for our bodies. Sadly, injury can make this extremely challenging.

Injury frequently leaves individuals with an extremely touchy caution framework in their bodies. The people who experienced sexual maltreatment as youngsters, for instance, find that they experience devastating frenzy in innocuous circumstances, like nestling with their accomplices.

To stay away from this, damaged individuals frequently endeavor to numb their sentiments by drinking excessively, ingesting medications, and even over-burdening themselves with work. These give a brief arrangement, however, will generally cause more damage than anything else to an individual's psychological well-being. Fortunately, there's a sound method for adapting to overpowering feelings in the outcome of injury: yoga.

For injury victims, yoga offers a protected method for reaching out to their feelings and comprehending how the body encounters them. Annie, one of the creator's patients, chose to check it out. As an assault casualty and PTSD victim, the main yoga classes were staggeringly challenging for her. Indeed, even a delicate congratulatory gesture could set off her mind's caution framework.

Notwithstanding this, Annie stayed with yoga, declining to surrender. Before adequately long, she saw that her body was continually conveying her messages about her profound state. Specifically, Annie battled with the yoga position of the "blissful child," which expects you to lie on your back with your knees bowed and your feet up in the air.

However Annie felt unimaginable agony, weakness, and bitterness in places like these, but she didn't drive those sentiments away, deciding to investigate and acknowledge them all things considered. Yoga assisted Annie with finding some peace with negative sensations like these and assisted her with the understanding that she could manage them head-on, instead of quelling them.

Key Lessons

- Yoga offers injury victims a protected method for investigating the connection between their body and brain.
- Injury frequently leaves individuals with an extremely touchy caution framework in their bodies.
- There's a sound method for adapting to overpowering feelings in the outcome of injury: yoga.
- Our body and psyche share a cozy relationship.
- To live a fair, stable life, we want to comprehend how our feelings work, and what they mean for our bodies.

Key Ideas from this section in your own words

_____
_____
_____
_____
_____
_____

Self-Reflection Questions

Draw out two questions from this section of the book and provide answers to the questions based on your study.

Question 1:
....
....

Answer_____
_____
_____
_____
_____
_____

Question 2:
....
....

Answer _____

_____
_____
_____
_____
_____
_____
_____

Action Plan

How do you intend to put the lessons from this section of the book into practice to improve your life?

_____
_____
_____
_____
_____
_____
_____
_____
_____
_____

TAKING CARE

Care and steady connections are crucial for injury recuperation.

Care is an in-vogue idea at this moment, yet it's not only a craze - it's an extraordinarily successful direction for living. It likewise comprises an incredible asset for injury recuperation, yet how can it work?

Care is tied in with keeping a cognizant consciousness of your body and your feelings, as opposed to denying them. This is particularly intense after injury, as agonizing recollections make us quell our feelings instead of addressing them.

Not even one of us likes to feel miserable, furious, or broken, particularly when these sentiments are set off by recollections of injury. However, by driving these sentiments away, you likewise lose the potential chance to defy your injury and begin the mending system.

Care can lighten the mental and physiological effects of injury, from misery to stress to psychosomatic circumstances like constant agony. It can likewise work on insusceptible reactions, initiate areas of the cerebrum that assist with managing feelings, and equilibrium out pressure chemical levels.

Besides care, strong individual connections are imperative in making a course for recuperation from injury. By building an organization of relatives, companions, and emotional wellness experts, patients can guarantee they generally have somebody to go to when they need assistance. These organizations can be framed through AA gatherings, strict gatherings, and veterans' associations, to give some examples.

Key Lessons

- Care is an in-vogue idea at this moment, yet it's not only a craze - it's an extraordinarily successful direction for living.
- Care is tied in with keeping a cognizant consciousness of your body and your feelings, as opposed to denying them.
- Besides care, strong individual connections are imperative in making a course for recuperation from injury.
- By building an organization of relatives, companions, and emotional wellness experts, patients can guarantee they generally have somebody to go to when they need assistance.

Key Ideas from this section in your own words

_____
_____
_____
_____
_____
_____

Self-Reflection Questions

Draw out two questions from this section of the book and provide answers to the questions based on your study.

Question 1:
....
....

Answer_____

_____
_____
_____
_____
_____

Question 2:

Answer

Action Plan

How do you intend to put the lessons from this section of the book into practice to improve your life?

_____
_____
_____
_____
_____
_____
_____
_____
_____
_____

NEUROFEEDBACK

Neurofeedback assists injury victims with revamping their minds. Did you have any idea that electrical signs are answerable for basically all that happens in your cerebrum? These mind waves administer our manners of thinking, so they're very significant. Tragically, they can likewise be harmed by injury. How about we figure out how?

There is a wide range of kinds of cerebrum waves, one of these being alpha waves, which are set off when we feel without a care in the world. A new report at the University of Adelaide in Australia inspected fighters who served in Iraq or Afghanistan and uncovered that the more they spent in the disaster area, the fewer alpha waves their minds delivered. All things being equal, warriors created cerebrum waves like those of youngsters determined to have ADHD, hampering their capacity to unwind, keep even-tempered, and center.

Luckily, the mind can recuperate. How? Through a cycle called neurofeedback.

Neurofeedback permits damaged individuals to change the cerebrum waves they produce, and energize the development of alpha waves to help them unwind and try to avoid panicking. By showing the patient's brainwaves to them progressively on a screen, they can see when they need to put forth a cognizant attempt to unwind. When they do, they'll see their alpha waves being delivered and even be compensated through a connection point that can feel like a computer game.

Take Lisa, a 27-year-elderly person and one of the creator's patients. Lisa's dad deserted the family when she was three, and her mom was harmful and savage. Lisa took off from home two times and elapsed through a few

encouraging homes, mental clinics, and, surprisingly, invested energy residing in the city.

Long periods of injury left Lisa with solid foolish desires. She'd hurt herself and obliterate the things around her, with little capacity to control her feelings. In any case, when she started neurofeedback treatment, things changed decisively. With her newly discovered capacity to create alpha waves and intentionally make herself unwind, Lisa had the option to discuss and manage the awful accidents from her young life.

Although neurofeedback has been demonstrated very compelling, it's still seldom applied. By and large, our general public has far to go concerning understanding and managing injury. Be that as it may, with a more extensive acknowledgment of care and further developed information about psychological maladjustments lately, there is a valid justification to be hopeful about the fate of emotional well-being treatment.

Key Lessons

- Neurofeedback assists injury victims with revamping their minds.
- There is a wide range of kinds of cerebrum waves, one of these being alpha waves, which are set off when we feel without a care in the world.
- Our general public has a long way to go concerning understanding and managing injury.
- By showing the patient's brainwaves to them progressively on a screen, they can see when they need to put forth a cognizant attempt to unwind.

Key Ideas from this section in your own words

_____
_____
_____
_____
_____

Self-Reflection Questions

Draw out two questions from this section of the book and provide answers to the questions based on your study.

Question 1:
....
....

Answer_____
_____
_____
_____
_____

Question 2:
....
....

Answer_____

Action Plan

How do you intend to put the lessons from this section of the book into practice to improve your life?

_____
_____
_____
_____
_____
_____
_____
_____
_____
_____

CONCLUSION

Even though injury can happen to anybody, very few of us know what horrible encounters mean for our psychological and actual well-being, even a long time after the occasion. Care, encouraging groups of people, EMDR, yoga, and new procedures like neurofeedback are fundamental apparatuses for injury victims as they figure out how to acknowledge, adapt to and recuperate from their injury.

Final Self-Evaluation Questions

1. What was the key reason you bought the book "The Power of One More"?

_____
_____
_____
_____

2. To what extent could you say you achieved your objectives?

_____
_____
_____
_____

3. Following what you've learned, what actions/behaviors should you start taking/doing?

_____
_____
_____
_____
_____
_____

4. What actions/behaviors should you stop doing?

_____
_____

_____
_____

5. Do you think you could possibly improve following what you learned from this book? What makes you think so?

_____
_____
_____
_____
_____
_____
_____

Printed in Great Britain
by Amazon